WILLIAM HENRY HARRISON

OUR NINTH PRESIDENT

by Ann Graham Gaines

THE CHILD'S WORLD®

Published in the United States of America

The Child's World®
1980 Lookout Drive • Mankato, MN 56003-1705
800-599-READ • www.childsworld.com

Acknowledgments
The Child's World®: Mary Berendes, Publishing Director

The Creative Spark: Mary McGavic, Project Director and Page Production;
Shari Joffe, Editorial Director; Deborah Goodsite, Photo Research

The Design Lab: Kathleen Petelinsek, Design

Content Advisers: James Curtis and Tammy Radcliff, Berkeley Plantation, Charles
City, Virginia

Photos
Cover and page 3: White House Historical Association (White House Collection),
(detail); White House Historical Association (White House Collection)

Interior: The Art Archive: 36 and 39 (Culver Pictures); Art Resource, NY: 23,
24, 35 (National Portrait Gallery, Smithsonian Institution); The Bridgeman
Art Library: 7 (Capitol Collection, Washington, USA), 12 (Private Collection,
Bonhams, London, UK), 17, 21, 27 (Private Collection, Peter Newark American
Pictures), 20 (Collection of the New-York Historical Society, USA); Corbis: 32
(Bettmann); The Granger Collection, New York: 4, 6, 8, 10, 11, 14 and 38, 16
and 38, 25, 28, 33 and 39, 37; Indiana Historical Bureau, State of Indiana: 30
(Governors' Portrait Collection); iStockphoto: 44 (Tim Fan); North Wind Picture
Archives: 15, 19 (North Wind); U.S. Air Force photo: 45; Virginia Department of
Historic Resources: 5.

Library of Congress Cataloging-in-Publication Data
Gaines, Ann.
  William Henry Harrison / by Ann Graham Gaines.
    p. cm. — (Presidents of the U.S.A.)
  Includes bibliographical references and index.
  ISBN 978-1-60253-038-6 (library bound : alk. paper)
  1. Harrison, William Henry, 1773–1841—Juvenile literature. 2. Presidents—
United States—Biography—Juvenile literature. I. Title.
  E392.G349 2008
  973.8'6'092—dc21
  [B]

                              2007042604

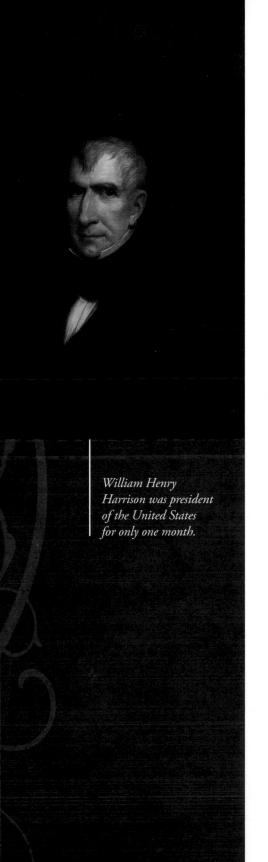

William Henry
Harrison was president
of the United States
for only one month.

TABLE OF CONTENTS

CHAPTER ONE

EARLY DAYS

William Henry Harrison was the ninth president of the United States. When he ran for president in 1840, he had already had a very long political career. He had first been elected to Congress more than forty years earlier. What no one realized was that his career would very soon come to a sudden halt. William Henry Harrison died just one month after being sworn in as president.

William Henry Harrison was born on February 9, 1773, on a plantation, or large farm, in Charles City County, Virginia. His parents, Benjamin and Elizabeth Harrison, were rich and powerful people. The Harrison family was among the most important families in what was then the colony of Virginia.

William Henry was the youngest of seven children. His family lived in luxury. Their home was a mansion with 22 rooms, each one filled with fancy furniture.

William Henry Harrison was the nation's ninth president. He had the misfortune of being the first president to die in office.

The children did not go to school because their family hired a **tutor** who taught them at their home.

Benjamin Harrison was a planter, a person who owns a plantation. He earned money selling crops that were raised on his farm. But he did not do farm work himself. Instead, he owned many slaves. They worked in his fields growing tobacco, cotton, and vegetables. Slaves did all the work in the Harrisons' house, too. They cooked, cleaned, and even sewed clothing for the family.

Benjamin Harrison was a very important figure in Virginia **politics.** When William Henry was born, his

William Henry Harrison was born at Berkeley Plantation, the beautiful estate that his grandfather built in 1726. It is located in Virginia on the James River. George Washington and each of the next nine presidents visited the plantation.

*Benjamin Harrison, William Henry's father, started the family **tradition** of being involved in politics. He was the governor of Virginia three times.*

William Henry Harrison was the last president born before the start of the American Revolution.

Harrison was the second president whose father had signed the Declaration of Independence. John Quincy Adams was the first. Adams's father not only signed that important document, he also became the nation's second president.

father had been a member of Virginia's **legislature** for 24 years.

The **American Revolution** began when William Henry was just two years old. The American colonies fought this war to win their independence from Great Britain. It lasted for six difficult years. Harrison thought it was exciting to grow up during the Revolution. He probably liked to watch soldiers march by and hear bands play **patriotic** songs.

Benjamin Harrison was a patriot. In 1775, he left Virginia's legislature after he was elected to the Continental Congress. During the time of the Revolution, the Continental Congress governed all the colonies. Its members met in Philadelphia, Pennsylvania. This kept Benjamin Harrison away from home for long periods of time. In 1776, the Continental Congress asked Thomas Jefferson to write the **Declaration of Independence.** When he finished, all the members of Congress signed it, including Benjamin Harrison. The Declaration of Independence announced that a new country was born—the United States of America.

Benjamin Harrison went back to his plantation after the American Revolution ended. There he continued as a member of Virginia's legislature until he was elected governor of the state. He served three **terms.** The Harrison children liked having their father home again after the war was over. While Benjamin was away, the family's tutor had taught William Henry to read and write. He also taught mathematics and

languages such as Greek and Latin. William Henry learned about politics and government from his father. He was a smart boy. At the age of 14, he enrolled at Hampden-Sydney College.

William Henry did not stay at the college long enough to graduate. His father wanted him to become a doctor. He sent William to study medicine with Benjamin Rush, a famous doctor in Philadelphia.

In 1791, Benjamin Harrison died. In those days, when a rich man died, he almost always left his fortune to his oldest son. In this case, William Henry Harrison's older brothers inherited their father's money. By this point, he already knew that he did not, in fact, want to be a doctor. He decided to become a soldier.

William Henry's father was one of the men who signed the Declaration of Independence. In this famous painting of the event by John Trumbull, Benjamin Harrison is the man seated at left in the red coat.

The Northwest Ordinance of 1787 created a new territory in what was then considered the West. The Northwest Territory stretched from Pennsylvania all the way to the Mississippi River.

On August 16, 1791, at age 18, William Henry joined the army as an officer, a person who commands soldiers in the army. There was no war at the time. But the army was still very active. Americans had begun to settle the Northwest **Territory.** After the American Revolution, some states that are small today were actually quite big. Connecticut, Massachusetts, and New York all owned land to the west. These lands stretched as far as the Mississippi River. All three states gave up most of their western land to the **federal** government in the 1780s.

In 1787, Congress passed the Northwest **Ordinance.** This law made the government's new western lands into the Northwest Territory. The ordinance said that when the population became large enough, the territory could break up into smaller territories. Then those territories could become new states. More and more settlers moved into these areas over the next 10 years. Some people became farmers. Others opened stores and offices in new towns that were founded all around the territory.

The Northwest Territory would later be split up and become the states of Ohio, Indiana, Illinois, Michigan, and Wisconsin. It was on the **frontier.** Beyond it lay wild land populated only by Native Americans. In the 1790s, the army's main responsibility was to protect settlers on the frontier from Native American attacks. Sometimes groups of Native Americans killed settlers or burned their houses. What the Native Americans really wanted to do was scare the settlers away. They wanted to take back the land that had belonged to them for centuries.

In Philadelphia, Harrison **recruited** 80 other men to join the army. They formed a company of soldiers, which he commanded. The army ordered Harrison and his men to march west over the Allegheny Mountains to a fort on the Ohio River. Today the city of Cincinnati, Ohio, is located there.

Harrison was the only president who had studied to become a doctor.

General Anthony Wayne (on white horse) and his troops defeated Native Americans at the Battle of Fallen Timbers. William Henry Harrison took part in this 1794 battle.

George Washington and his family were friends of the Harrisons. When William Henry Harrison joined the army, it was George Washington who signed the papers making him an officer.

Fort Washington was commanded by General "Mad Anthony" Wayne. General Wayne liked Harrison so much that he soon gave him a promotion. Within a year, he'd made him his aide. Harrison was a soldier in the army for almost seven years. He and his men built new forts. In 1794, they won the Battle of Fallen Timbers. After that, there were few problems with Native Americans in that area. One year later, General Wayne died. Harrison took over his command. Harrison was a brave man who was skilled at shooting a gun and commanding soldiers.

While in the army, Harrison met Anna Symmes, whose family had just moved to the area. They started spending time with each other, but her father did not

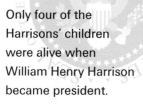

like the young officer. One day while Anna's father was away on business, they married in secret.

Anna's father feared that Harrison would not be able to support a family. He worried that Harrison's work was too risky and that he might be killed one day. In fact, the Harrisons would be married for close to fifty years. Together, they had 10 children. Sadly, six of their children did not survive past childhood.

Only four of the Harrisons' children were alive when William Henry Harrison became president.

Anna Symmes Harrison was as independent as her husband. When her parents refused to let her marry William Henry, she decided to **elope.** *Over the years, her husband was often away, so she cared for their family and home by herself.*

THANKSGIVING

When Americans celebrate Thanksgiving, they're remembering a date in 1621 when the Plymouth colonists and the Wampanoag Indians met for an autumn feast. What few people know is that that was not in fact the first Thanksgiving to be held in what would become the United States. In 1619, English settlers came ashore at what would one day be Berkeley Plantation, William Henry Harrison's childhood home. They had their own Thanksgiving on December 4, offering prayers celebrating their safe arrival in the New World. In years to come, the occasion would always be remembered and celebrated at Berkeley.

CHAPTER TWO

LIFE IN INDIANA

In 1798, William Henry Harrison left the army. He wanted to become a farmer, but he and his wife did not want to move back to his home state of Virginia. They wanted to stay on the frontier. So Harrison bought 160 acres of land to farm. It was located on the Ohio River, 14 miles south of where Cincinnati is today. Farming was not all Harrison planned to do, however. Now 25 years old, he had many goals. Most of all, he wanted to become a powerful **politician** like his father had been.

On June 29, 1798, he began his career in politics. His father-in-law was a powerful judge who had friends in Washington, D.C. He persuaded John Adams to ask Congress to name William Henry Harrison the secretary of the Northwest Territory.

As secretary, Harrison kept records for the government. In 1799, he left that position. He was elected the territory's **representative** to the United States Congress. Harrison left his family behind and went to Philadelphia, then the nation's capital.

In Congress, he often spoke up for westerners. He wanted to make sure they got their share of the

*The Harrisons built
a lovely home (in
background) on their
land, which overlooked
the Ohio River.*

federal government's money. He wanted roads and
waterways built in the West, not just in the East. One
of Harrison's most important achievements while in
Congress was introducing the Land Act of 1800. This
law lowered the price families paid to buy small plots
of land in the West. It meant more people could move
to the frontier and begin new lives.

In 1800, Congress passed a law that divided the
Northwest Territory. Harrison became governor of
the part that became the territory of Indiana. He and

his family then went to live in Vincennes, the capital of Indiana at the time. He was governor for 12 years, from January of 1801 to December of 1812. He helped establish the territory's legislature and chose other officials to help him run the new government. He also made sure that Indiana's roads were improved.

The biggest challenge that Harrison faced as governor was dealing with Native Americans. Settlers wanted to take over more and more Native American land. President John Adams and then President Thomas Jefferson ordered Harrison to secure claims to the Native Americans' land so that settlers could live on it. Harrison knew the settlers were taking away the Native Americans' rights. The settlers were also

Thousands of people settled in the Northwest Territory. They were excited at the prospect of starting new lives on the frontier. Harrison wanted to help these settlers. He helped get a law passed that lowered the price of land in the West.

Tecumseh was a great Shawnee Indian chief. Once he arrived at a battle just in time to see Native Americans brutally killing their American prisoners. Tecumseh scolded the warriors and stopped the violence. This event strengthened the great chief's **reputation** among Native Americans and Americans alike.

treating the Native Americans badly. But Harrison believed that the rights of settlers, not those of the Native Americans, were his responsibility. As governor, he met with Native American chiefs. He convinced these leaders to give up a huge amount of land to the American government. Sometimes the government paid the Native Americans for their land, but even then it was only a very small amount of money.

Between 1802 and 1805, Harrison signed seven treaties with Native Americans. Over time, they gave

William Henry Harrison was the first congressman ever elected from Indiana. He was also the first governor of the territory of Indiana.

Tenskwatawa (left), the brother of Tecumseh, was a religious and political leader of the Shawnee people. He believed that white peoples' ways were a destructive influence on his people.

up more than 50 million acres. Many Native Americans did not like what was happening. Some British people living in Canada encouraged the Native Americans to fight the settlers. Two brothers named Tecumseh and Tenskwatawa belonged to the Shawnee tribe. They wanted to help Native Americans end the invasion by white people.

Tecumseh formed a **confederation** of tribes. He convinced Native American people from as far away as Canada and Florida to join forces. Fighting together, they would have a better chance in battles against the

William Henry Harrison had more grandchildren (48) and great-grandchildren (106) than any other president.

settlers. Tenskwatawa, whom Americans called "The Prophet," tried to help Native Americans bring back their traditions. He wanted them to stop buying goods such as rifles and alcohol from white people. He said they should live as their ancestors had.

Together, the members of Tecumseh's confederation owned a great deal of land. Harrison tried to get Tecumseh to agree to sell the government their land in Indiana. He offered $10,000, but Tecumseh refused. He told Harrison that "the Americans had driven them from the sea coast." What Tecumseh meant was that his people had been pushed out of places such as Virginia and Massachusetts by white settlers. Tecumseh predicted that Americans "would shortly, if not stopped, push them into the [Great] Lakes."

In 1809, Harrison **negotiated** the **Treaty** of Fort Wayne, an agreement between the United States and many different Native American tribes. Harrison didn't invite Tecumseh's tribe and other hostile tribes to the meeting, even though earlier treaties had said that the land being discussed belonged to those tribes. Instead, Harrison met with members of the Delaware, Miami, Potawatomi, and Eel tribes. They agreed to give the United States three million acres of land. Harrison offered them not quite two cents for each acre of land.

Tecumseh had already begun to bring together a large group of warriors. He was trying to build a powerful Native American army. Now he tried to talk the British into joining him in his fight against the American settlers. Harrison wrote to Tecumseh, warning him he would not be able to win against the Americans. In 1810, Tecumseh and a large group of warriors came to try to talk to Harrison and other officials at Harrison's home. The meeting ended with shouting. Swords, pistols, and war clubs were brandished. Fighting didn't actually break out, but no agreement was reached, either.

Tecumseh's warriors built a town on Tippecanoe Creek. Settlers were fearful of what would happen next. In 1811, President James Madison authorized a raid against the Native Americans. Despite the fact that Harrison had left the army 13 years earlier, he was given command of a large number of soldiers and

In 1810, Tecumseh went to Harrison's home to try to work out a peace agreement. He lost his temper, however, when Harrison refused to undo the Treaty of Fort Wayne, which had taken a great deal of land away from the Shawnee.

Settlers in the West viewed the Battle of Tippecanoe as a great victory against the Native Americans. Harrison's actions made him a hero to people all around the country. The battle was so famous in the United States that Harrison was nicknamed "Old Tippecanoe."

militiamen. Harrison led 800 soldiers into battle, even though he was still the governor. He said he planned to deal the tribes "a sweeping blow" by destroying their town by the creek.

As it turned out, Tecumseh was away. Tenskwatawa was in charge. He launched a surprise attack on the Americans early in the morning. "Indians were in the Camp before many of my men could get out of their tents," Harrison later wrote. Sixty-one American soldiers died and 127 were wounded in the Battle of Tippecanoe. After Harrison rallied his men, many Native Americans died as well. Finally, the tribes were forced to flee. The U.S. soldiers who were not hurt in battle moved on to burn the Native American village. With that, they could claim a victory.

TECUMSEH

Before the Battle of Tippecanoe, the Shawnee people had attacked whites who moved onto their lands for many years. Tecumseh, whose father had been a war chief, fought in his first battle when he was just nine years old. By the time he was 20, he had become famous not only as a fierce warrior, but also as a man of intelligence. He knew many Native American languages, as well as English and French.

Tecumseh traveled hundreds of miles east of the Mississippi River, forming a confederation of Native American tribes. He explained that tribes had to protect their way of life, or it would be destroyed forever. To do this, every tribe had to join together. Many Native Americans accepted him as their leader. His confederation eventually included 50 tribes. They promised to stop fighting each other and to fight the Americans together.

Tecumseh built a powerful Native American army. It fought on the side of the British in the War of 1812. In exchange, the British promised that they would give the Native Americans what is now Michigan at the end of the war. But this did not happen. Tecumseh died at the Battle of the Thames on October 5, 1813. The alliance broke up after his death.

CHAPTER THREE

A LONG POLITICAL LIFE

News of the Battle of Tippecanoe spread quickly beyond Indiana to the East Coast. Although some criticized William Henry Harrison's actions, many Americans decided he was a hero. A well-known congressman named Henry Clay wrote to Harrison, saying that he admired him and his courage. In the years that followed, Clay became Harrison's friend and helped him in his political career.

Not all Americans believed Harrison's actions were right, however. Some politicians accused him of "horrible butchery." They said that too many Americans had died in the battle. Unfortunately, few politicians were concerned about the Native American lives that were lost.

Harrison's victory in the Battle of Tippecanoe did not help Americans solve their problems with Native Americans. In 1812, war broke out between the United States and Great Britain. Tecumseh and his warriors wanted revenge against Americans. They became the **allies** of Great Britain, fighting alongside British soldiers.

Congressman Henry Clay admired Harrison's actions during the Battle of Tippecanoe. He recommended that the army make Harrison a general and give him more responsibility.

The situation in the Northwest Territory was not good for Americans. The British seized control of a lot of American land. They captured and burned the city of Detroit.

In August of 1812, Governor Harrison rejoined the army once more. Henry Clay persuaded army officials to make him a general, one of the army's most important commanders. The following year, Clay convinced Congress to give Harrison command of a large group of soldiers, called the Northwestern Army.

In December of 1812, Harrison's term as governor of Indiana ended. He decided to stay in the army. He

Even after the War of 1812, warfare against Native Americans raged on for many years. The United States was determined to control the land from coast to coast.

fought with all his might during the War of 1812. Twice British soldiers surrounded his men, putting them under **siege.** The Americans could not leave their camp. They became very hungry because they ran out of supplies. Still, they held on. Finally, the British gave up and left them alone.

Harrison was named a general after the Battle of Tippecanoe. Generals are the most important officers in the army.

In the fall of 1813, the American navy won a huge battle and won back control of Lake Erie. Now the British could no longer send supplies to their soldiers based in Michigan and Canada.

Harrison and his men were sent to try to win back the city of Detroit for the United States. After they succeeded, they set out to chase down the enemy. On October 5, 1813, Harrison's men beat a large group of Native American warriors and British soldiers in the Battle of the Thames. Tecumseh died in that battle. After Tecumseh's death, the confederation he had founded fell apart. Native Americans no longer challenged American settlers' claim to the northwestern lands.

Harrison and his men were victorious at the Battle of the Thames on October 5, 1813. Tecumseh died in the battle. Without the chief's leadership, the Native American confederation fell apart.

In 1818, Congress voted to give Harrison a gold medal for the courage he displayed as a soldier in the War of 1812.

The battle also greatly benefited William Henry Harrison personally. His reputation as a hero was cemented. Instead of fighting on, he decided to take a leave from the army and go on a tour of important American cities, including New York, Philadelphia, and Washington. Everywhere he went, celebrations were held in his honor. In May of 1814, Harrison retired from the army. He was 41 years old.

Over the next 25 years, Harrison tended his farm. He also ran for many political offices, but often didn't win. He kept running for office partly because he wanted the salary the government pays its politicians. It cost Harrison a great deal of money to raise his large family. But it wasn't just the money that drew him into races. He also really enjoyed politics. For many years, Harrison belonged to the Democratic-Republican **political party,** which had been started years before by Thomas Jefferson and other founding fathers.

From 1816 to 1819, Harrison represented Indiana in the U.S. House of Representatives. From 1819 to 1821, he served in the Ohio State Senate. His land sat on the border between the territories of Ohio and Indiana, so he could serve in both states. Twice he ran in Ohio for election as U.S. senator. He lost both times. Several times, he ran for election as governor of Ohio, but he never won. He hoped President James Monroe would name him secretary of war, but that did not happen. In 1822, he made an unsuccessful bid to return to the U.S. House of Representatives.

Andrew Jackson was another hero from the War of 1812. When he became president in 1829, he removed all of his political enemies from government positions—including William Henry Harrison. The Whig Party was formed to fight Jackson and his followers.

In 1824, Harrison finally won a U.S. Senate seat. As senator, he had a very important job. He was in charge of the committee on military affairs. He was also a supporter of the president, John Quincy Adams. In 1828, Adams rewarded Harrison for his loyalty by making him a diplomat. He was sent to serve as an **ambassador** to the South American country of Colombia. The next year, Democrat Andrew Jackson became president. Jackson hated Adams and his allies, including Harrison. He took away Harrison's job so he could give it to one of his own supporters.

Harrison returned from Colombia in September of 1829. He returned to the task of tending his farm.

Anna Harrison did not want her husband to run for president in the elections of 1836 and 1840. She wanted "Pa," as she called him, to stay home and work on the family farm.

He also changed political parties. He was so angry at the way Andrew Jackson had treated him, he left the Democratic Party. He joined the new Whig Party. This political party was formed to oppose Jackson's Democrats.

In 1834, Harrison took a job keeping records for the county court to earn extra money. One year later, he decided to run for the most important office in the nation. He began to **campaign** for the 1836 presidential election. President Jackson wanted another Democrat, Martin Van Buren, to succeed him. The Whigs thought that people would elect William Henry Harrison because he was another war hero, like Jackson. The Whigs also ran three other **candidates,** each one representing a different region. The hoped that this strategy would prevent Van Buren from receiving enough votes to win. Harrison was their western candidate.

This political cartoon about the 1836 presidential election shows "Old Tippecanoe" (on the right) fighting with the Democratic presidential candidate, Martin Van Buren.

THE SHORTEST PRESIDENCY

In 1836, Americans were celebrating the 25th anniversary of the Battle of Tippecanoe. When people told the story of what had happened there, they described William Henry Harrison as a hero. Harrison received the most votes in nine states. But he lost the presidential election of 1836. Democrat Martin Van Buren won the vote in even more states. He became the president in 1837.

Van Buren's term as president would not be an easy one. He inherited many problems from Andrew Jackson. During the Panic of 1837, many people lost their jobs and businesses, and banks failed.

The Whigs were disappointed that Van Buren became the new president. They immediately set to work, planning to win the next election. For years, the Democrats had claimed to be the party of the people. This meant that they represented working people, such as farmers and shopkeepers, instead of rich people. But the Whigs usually helped wealthy businessmen and Southern plantation owners. Now the Whigs realized the votes of ordinary working people were important,

The Whigs were determined to win the election of 1840. They portrayed William Harrison as a common man, thinking this would appeal to many Americans.

Political rallies were fun and exciting when Harrison ran against Martin Van Buren. Bands played music while people cheered. The Whigs put out hard cider for everyone to drink.

too. They wanted to attract the votes of laborers, farmers, and frontiersmen.

Leaders of the Whig Party thought Harrison could beat Van Buren in the next presidential election. They asked Harrison to run and began to create a positive image for him. They praised him as a war hero. To make him seem like a regular person, they said Harrison lived on the frontier in a log cabin. They said he liked to drink hard cider, which is a drink made from apples, instead of expensive wines from foreign countries. The Whigs hoped this would increase Harrison's appeal to ordinary Americans.

Harrison's supporters also told lies about Van Buren. Whig newspaper editors criticized the president. They said Van Buren was a dandy, a man who is too concerned about his appearance. They claimed he loved to look at himself in mirrors!

Americans were arguing over some very big issues. The country was beginning to divide over the issue of whether to outlaw slavery. Many people who lived in the North wanted it ended in all the states. But Southerners depended on slaves to work on their plantations. They believed ending slavery would ruin their **economy.** Americans also disagreed over tariffs, which are taxes placed on goods brought in from foreign countries. For years, they had been arguing over whether to have a national bank that controlled all the government's money. Some leaders wanted to distribute the money among many smaller banks instead of giving so much power to a single large one.

Whig Party leaders ordered Harrison not to speak out about topics such as slavery, tariffs, and the U.S. bank system. They didn't want him to lose votes by expressing an unpopular opinion.

Harrison traveled all over delivering speeches. People turned out in great numbers for his rallies, which were large celebrations held to show support for him. Harrison easily won the election of 1840.

He traveled by train to Washington, D.C., becoming the first president to arrive by rail for his **inauguration.** He was sworn in on March 4, 1841. Anna Harrison was sick when her husband was elected. She could not go to Washington with him at first. Unfortunately, her husband would die before she arrived in the capital city.

The day of Harrison's inauguration was cold and wet. The ceremony took place outside. To get there, Harrison rode a horse. He wore no hat or coat. Then he stood in the icy rain for more than two hours. It took him that long to read his inaugural address, the speech the president gives to the public on inauguration day.

Throughout his campaign, he had avoided speaking out on many issues. Now he spelled out exactly what he wanted to accomplish as president. He planned to let Congress take the lead. He criticized earlier presidents for having seized powers that weren't supposed to be theirs. On the matter of slavery, he was very clear—he supported states' rights, thinking each state ought to be allowed to decide whether to

At one rally in Tippecanoe, 60,000 fans came out to see William Henry Harrison.

In the election of 1840, William Henry Harrison won four times as many votes as his opponent, Martin Van Buren.

Harrison's inauguration took place on a terribly cold day. Still, he gave a very long speech. In fact, it was the longest inaugural address ever given.

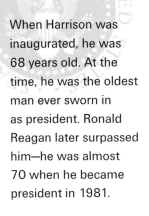

When Harrison was inaugurated, he was 68 years old. At the time, he was the oldest man ever sworn in as president. Ronald Reagan later surpassed him—he was almost 70 when he became president in 1981.

allow slavery within its boundaries. He promised not to interfere in military affairs. The crowd in attendance was larger than any since George Washington had been sworn in some 50 years before.

Later, Harrison went out walking from reception to reception. He was caught in a rainstorm. He was drenched, but did not change his clothes. That evening, he said he did not feel very well, but he started working right away the next morning. Over the next two weeks, he made many political **appointments,** assigning people to important government positions. Thousands of people wrote or came to ask Harrison for a job. "The job seekers pack the White House every day," he said. But he did not want to be a puppet that just did what members of his political party wanted. In fact, Harrison's cabinet, the group of men who helped him to make decisions, wanted him to appoint someone he did not respect as the governor of Iowa. Harrison refused to give in to their pressure.

In late March, doctors said the president had **pneumonia** and ordered him to bed. Doctors tried "modern" treatments, such as applying heated cups to

William Henry Harrison died on April 4, a month after his inauguration. His presidency was the shortest in American history.

33

his skin to draw out the disease. They even tried traditional Native American cures.

Newspapers did not report that Harrison was sick until March 31. By this time he was very weak, and his wife was still in Ohio. Anna received a message telling her that her husband was sick. But she did not arrive in time to see Harrison before he died on April 4, 1841. Vice President John Tyler had also been away. He did not know until the next day that Harrison had died.

Americans were shocked when newspapers announced the president's death. People gathered on street corners and in shops to talk about the sad event. They wondered what would happen next. In Washington, businesses and offices shut down. Government buildings were draped in black fabric as a sign of respect and sorrow for the president.

Harrison's body lay at the White House. He was honored with an official funeral. Important people crowded into the East Room of the White House to pay their respects. After officials spoke, men carried out his coffin and placed it on a wagon painted black. A band played **dirges,** very sad songs that are played at funerals. A large group of people followed the wagon to the Congressional Cemetery. Later that month, Harrison's coffin was taken by train to Ohio, where it was buried.

For a short time, no one was sure what to do. Should the United States swear in a new president right away? Should it wait for a time to show respect for President Harrison? There were also questions about who should become the president. But Vice President Tyler said

William Henry Harrison's grandson, Benjamin Harrison, was also a politician. He became the 23rd U.S. president in 1889.

that he should be made president. He quickly made arrangements to be sworn in.

Tyler's actions created the tradition that has always been followed when an American president dies in office. Today Americans know that there is always a chance the president will die during his term. They count on the government to keep working if this ever happens.

No one knows what kind of president Harrison would have been. Would he have helped his nation? The last words that Harrison spoke were said to his doctor. But perhaps they were meant for the person who would take over leadership. "Sir," said Harrison, "I wish you to understand the true **principles** of the government. I wish them carried out. I ask nothing more."

HARRISONIAN

BALL ROLLING.

KEEP THE

WILLIAM HENRY HARRISON THE FARMER OF NORTH BEND.

RALLY!

A General Meeting

Will be held at the Old COURT ROOM, [Riey's building]

On Saturday Evening,

The 18th instant, at early candle light.   A punctual attendance is requested.

MESSRS. DAVIS, BOTKIN, KEATING

And others, will address the Meeting.

July 17, 1840.   R. P. TODD, *Chairman*
                                  Vigilance Committee.

PRESIDENTIAL CAMPAIGNS

Today presidential campaigns last for more than a year.
Presidential candidates make many public appearances. They
give speeches and appear in television commercials. Voters have
many chances to find out who the candidates are and what they
plan to do if they become president.

George Washington and other early presidents did not
campaign. Voters chose presidents based on what they had
already accomplished. William Henry Harrison was the first
presidential candidate to campaign. He made appearances at
dozens of political rallies and picnics. People began calling
Harrison "Tippecanoe." During the 1840 presidential election,
Democrats shouted "Tippecanoe and Tyler, Too" at rallies to
signal their support for Harrison and the vice presidential
candidate, John Tyler. They even wrote songs praising Harrison
and Tyler and held parades in their honor. The poster shown here
features a log cabin, a symbol of Harrison's 1840 campaign.

DEATH IN THE HIGHEST OFFICE

Eight American presidents have died in office. William Henry Harrison was the first. In 1850, Zachary Taylor became the second president to die during his term. On April 14, 1865, in one of saddest events in American history, Abraham Lincoln (below) was **assassinated**. A Southerner named John Wilkes Booth was angry that the North had won the Civil War. Booth shot Lincoln at a theater, while the president was watching a play. Americans were shocked by the assassination, and they thought such a terrible thing could never happen again. They were wrong.

An insane man who believed he should have been given an important government position shot James Garfield. Garfield died September 19, 1881. William McKinley was shot by a man who wanted to overthrow the government. He died on September 14, 1901. In 1923, Warren G. Harding died from a sudden illness. Franklin D. Roosevelt served as president longer than any other. He faced two serious problems that left him frail and exhausted: the Great Depression and World War II. He died on April 12, 1945, soon after his fourth inauguration. The most recent president to die in office was John F. Kennedy, who was assassinated on November 22, 1963. Americans who were alive at the time will never forget the grief they felt when they heard the news.

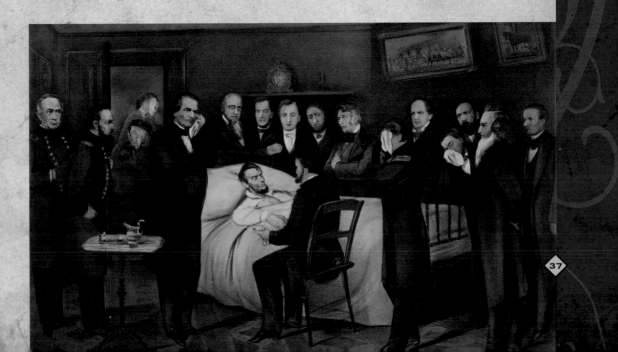

Time Line

1773
William Henry Harrison is born on February 9 on his family's Virginia plantation. His parents, Benjamin and Elizabeth, have seven children.

1775
The American Revolution begins.

1776
Benjamin Harrison, a member of the Continental Congress, signs the Declaration of Independence. The United States is born.

1788
Harrison enrolls at Hampden-Sydney College in Virginia. He is 14 years old.

1787
The U.S. Congress passes the Northwest Ordinance. This law creates the Northwest Territory from the government's western lands. Ohio, Indiana, Illinois, Michigan, and Wisconsin will later be formed out of the Territory.

1790
Harrison leaves college to begin studying medicine.

1791
Harrison decides he does not want to become a doctor. He briefly returns to Hampden-Sydney College before deciding to become a soldier. He joins the army as an officer. The army sends him and his company of soldiers to Ohio to help protect settlers on the frontier.

1795
Harrison marries Anna Symmes, whom he met in Ohio.

1798
On June 1, Harrison resigns from the army. He becomes secretary of the Northwest Territory.

1799
Harrison is elected to the U.S. House of Representatives.

1800
President John Adams appoints Harrison governor of the new Indiana Territory.

1801
Harrison begins his new job as governor of Indiana in January. He holds the position for 12 years.

1809
Harrison negotiates the Treaty of Fort Wayne with the Delaware, Miami, Potawatomi, and Eel tribes. The tribes agree to give the American government millions of acres of their land.

1810
Shawnee Chief Tecumseh starts to build a confederation of Native American tribes. He wants warriors to form an army to force settlers from Native American lands.

1811
Harrison leads soldiers in the Battle of Tippecanoe, against Tecumseh's soldiers, on November 11. The Americans win the battle.

1812
The War of 1812 begins. Harrison rejoins the army, even though he is still governor of Indiana. In December, his term as governor ends.

1813
Harrison is given command of the Northwestern Army. On October 5, he and his men fight the Battle of the Thames. Tecumseh dies in the battle.

1814
In May, Harrison retires from the army and goes home to his farm.

1816
Harrison is again elected to the U.S. House of Representatives.

1819
Harrison leaves the House of Representatives. He is then elected to the Ohio State Senate.

1821
Harrison leaves his seat in the Ohio Senate. He runs for governor of Ohio several times over the next few years but is not elected.

1825
The people of Ohio elect Harrison to the U.S. Senate.

1828
President John Quincy Adams appoints Harrison ambassador to Colombia, a country in South America. Harrison resigns his seat in the U.S. Senate to accept the position.

1829
Harrison comes home from Colombia. A new president, Andrew Jackson, has given the position to one of his own supporters.

1835
Harrison begins to campaign for the 1836 presidential election. He travels all over the Midwest to meet voters and give speeches.

1836
Harrison is praised as a war hero, but he does not win the election.

1838
Although the next presidential election is still two years away, leaders of the Whig Party discuss how to keep President Van Buren from being reelected. They ask Harrison to run against him.

1839
Harrison campaigns for election as president in what is called the Log Cabin Campaign. His opponent is again Martin Van Buren.

1840
Harrison defeats Martin Van Buren and is elected president.

1841
Harrison is inaugurated on March 4. The day of his inauguration is cold and wet, and he catches a cold. By the end of the month, he is very ill. On April 4, he dies of pneumonia. John Tyler becomes the nation's 10th president.

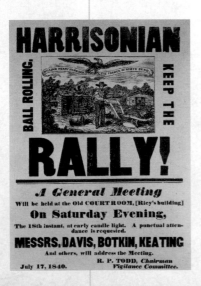

39

GLOSSARY

allies (AL-lize) Allies are people or nations that have agreed to help each other by fighting together against a common enemy. During the War of 1812, Native Americans were British allies.

ambassador (am-BASS-uh-dur) An ambassador is the top person sent by a government to represent it in another country. Harrison was made an ambassador to Colombia in 1828.

American Revolution (uh-MEHR-ih-kuhn rev-uh-LOO-shun) The American Revolution was the war in which the United States fought for its freedom from England. It began when Harrison was two years old.

appointments (uh-POYNT-ments) Appointments are important positions in the government to which a person is assigned by an official. President Harrison made political appointments to many positions.

assassinated (uh-SASS-ih-nayt-id) Assassinated means murdered, especially a well-known person. President Lincoln was assassinated in 1865.

campaign (kam-PAYN) A campaign is the process of running for an election, including activities such as giving speeches or attending rallies. Harrison was the first presidential candidate to campaign.

candidates (KAN-dih-detz) Candidates are people running in an election. Presidential candidates make many public appearances.

confederation (kun-fed-er-AY-shun) A confederation is a group of people who come together for a common purpose. Native American tribes formed a confederation to keep settlers from taking their lands.

Declaration of Independence (deh-kluh-RAY-shun OF in-dee-PEN-dens) The Declaration of Independence is a document that was written in 1776. It announced the independence of the United States from Great Britain.

dirges (DUR-jez) Dirges are slow, mournful pieces of music played during a person's funeral. A band played dirges at Harrison's funeral.

economy (ee-KON-uh-mee) An economy is the way money is earned and spent. Southerners believed that ending slavery would ruin their economy.

elope (eh-LOHP) When people elope, they run away to get married without letting others know about it. Anna and William Henry Harrison eloped.

federal (FED-er-ul) Federal means having to do with the central government of the United States, rather than a state or city government. Some states gave up their western lands to the federal government in the 1780s.

frontier (frun-TEER) A frontier is a region that is at the edge of or beyond settled land. The Northwest Territory was on the frontier.

inauguration (ih-nawg-yuh-RAY-shun) An inauguration is the ceremony that takes place when a new president begins a term. The day of Harrison's inauguration was cold and wet.

legislature (LEJ-ih-slay-chur) A legislature is the part of a government that makes laws. Harrison's father was a member of the Virginia legislature.

negotiated (nuh-GOH-shee-ay-tid) If people negotiated, they talked things over and tried to come to an agreement. Harrison negotiated a treaty with Native Americans in 1809.

ordinance (OR-dih-nuhnz) An ordinance is a an order or law. Congress passed the Northwest Ordinance to create the Northwest Territory.

patriotic (pay-tree-AH-tik) Patriotic means loving one's country. William Henry Harrison was patriotic.

pneumonia (nuh-MOH-nyuh) Pneumonia is a disease that causes swelling of the lungs, high fever, and difficulty breathing. President Harrison died of pneumonia.

political party (puh-LIT-ih-kul PAR-tee) A political party is a group of people who share similar ideas about how to run a government. Harrison was a member of the Democratic political party at one time.

politician (pawl-ih-TISH-un) A politician is a person who holds an office in government. Harrison wanted to be a politician like his father.

politics (PAWL-uh-tiks) Politics refers to the actions and practices of the government. Harrison had a long career in politics.

precedent (PRESS-uh-duhnt) A precedent is something done or said that becomes an example for the future. John Tyler set the precedent for the vice president becoming president when a president dies.

principles (PRIN-sih-puls) Principles are a people's basic beliefs, or what they believe to be right and true. Harrison hoped the president who followed him would understand the principles of the U.S. government.

rallies (RAL-eez) Rallies are large meetings. Political rallies were held during Harrison's campaign for president.

recruited (ree-KREWT-id) If people recruited others, they convinced them to join a group. Harrison recruited men to the army.

representative (rep-ree-ZEN-tuh-tiv) A representative is someone who attends a meeting, having agreed to speak or act for others. Harrison was the Northwest Territory's representative in the U.S. Congress in 1798.

reputation (rep-yoo-TAY-shun) A reputation is one's worth or character, as judged by other people. Tecumseh had a good reputation.

siege (SEEJ) If people or places are under siege, they have been surrounded or captured. The British put Harrison's men under siege during the War of 1812.

terms (TERMZ) Terms are the length of time politicians can keep their positions by law. A U.S. president's term of office is four years.

territory (TAYR-ih-tor-ee) A territory is a land or region, especially land that belongs to a government. A new law in 1787 created the Northwest Territory.

tradition (tra-DIH-shun) A tradition is a custom handed down from one generation to the next. Tenskwatawa tried to help Native Americans bring back their traditions.

treaty (TREE-tee) A treaty is a formal agreement made between groups or nations. Harrison helped negotiate the Treaty of Fort Wayne.

tutor (TOO-tur) A tutor is a teacher who gives private lessons. As a child, Harrison was schooled by a tutor.

THE UNITED STATES GOVERNMENT

The United States government is divided into three equal branches: the executive, the legislative, and the judicial. This division helps prevent abuses of power because each branch has to answer to the other two. No one branch can become too powerful.

EXECUTIVE BRANCH

PRESIDENT
VICE PRESIDENT
DEPARTMENTS

The job of the executive branch is to enforce the laws. It is headed by the president, who serves as the spokesperson for the United States around the world. The president signs bills into law and appoints important officials such as federal judges. He or she is also the commander in chief of the U.S. military. The president is assisted by the vice president, who takes over if the president dies or cannot carry out the duties of the office.

The executive branch also includes various departments, each focused on a specific topic. They include the Defense Department, the Justice Department, and the Agriculture Department. The department heads, along with other officials such as the vice president, serve as the president's closest advisers, called the cabinet.

LEGISLATIVE BRANCH

CONGRESS
Senate and
House of Representatives

The job of the legislative branch is to make the laws. It consists of Congress, which is divided into two parts: the Senate and the House of Representatives. The Senate has 100 members, and the House of Representatives has 435 members. Each state has two senators. The number of representatives a state has varies depending on the state's population.

Besides making laws, Congress also passes budgets and enacts taxes. In addition, it is responsible for declaring war, maintaining the military, and regulating trade with other countries.

JUDICIAL BRANCH

SUPREME COURT
COURTS OF APPEALS
DISTRICT COURTS

The job of the judicial branch is to interpret the laws. It consists of the nation's federal courts. Trials are held in district courts. During trials, judges must decide what laws mean and how they apply. Courts of appeals review the decisions made in district courts.

The nation's highest court is the Supreme Court. If someone disagrees with a court of appeals ruling, he or she can ask the Supreme Court to review it. The Supreme Court may refuse. The Supreme Court makes sure that decisions and laws do not violate the Constitution.

CHOOSING
THE PRESIDENT

It may seem odd, but American voters don't elect the president directly. Instead, the president is chosen using what is called the Electoral College.

Each state gets as many votes in the Electoral College as its combined total of senators and representatives in Congress. For example, Iowa has two senators and five representatives, so it gets seven electoral votes. Although the District of Columbia does not have any voting members in Congress, it gets three electoral votes. Usually, the candidate who wins the most votes in any given state receives all of that state's electoral votes.

To become president, a candidate must get more than half of the Electoral College votes. There are a total of 538 votes in the Electoral College, so a candidate needs 270 votes to win. If nobody receives 270 Electoral College votes, the House of Representatives chooses the president.

With the Electoral College system, the person who receives the most votes nationwide does not always receive the most electoral votes. This happened most recently in 2000, when Al Gore received half a million more national votes than George W. Bush. Bush became president because he had more Electoral College votes.

THE WHITE HOUSE

The White House is the official home of the president of the United States. It is located at 1600 Pennsylvania Avenue NW in Washington, D.C. In 1792, a contest was held to select the architect who would design the president's home. James Hoban won. Construction took eight years.

The first president, George Washington, never lived in the White House. The second president, John Adams, moved into the house in 1800, though the inside was not yet complete. During the War of 1812, British soldiers burned down much of the White House. It was rebuilt several years later.

The White House was changed through the years. Porches were added, and President Theodore Roosevelt added the West Wing. President William Taft changed the shape of the presidential office, making it into the famous Oval Office. While Harry Truman was president, the old house was discovered to be structurally weak. All the walls were reinforced with steel, and the rooms were rebuilt.

Today, the White House has 132 rooms (including 35 bathrooms), 28 fireplaces, and 3 elevators. It takes 570 gallons of paint to cover the outside of the six-story building. The White House provides the president with many ways to relax. It includes a putting green, a jogging track, a swimming pool, a tennis court, and beautifully landscaped gardens. The White House also has a movie theater, a billiard room, and a one-lane bowling alley.

PRESIDENTIAL PERKS

The job of president of the United States is challenging. It is probably one of the most stressful jobs in the world. Because of this, presidents are paid well, though not nearly as well as the leaders of large corporations. In 2007, the president earned $400,000 a year. Presidents also receive extra benefits that make the demanding job a little more appealing.

★ **Camp David:** In the 1940s, President Franklin D. Roosevelt chose this heavily wooded spot in the mountains of Maryland to be the presidential retreat, where presidents can relax. Even though it is a retreat, world business is conducted there. Most famously, President Jimmy Carter met with Middle Eastern leaders at Camp David in 1978. The result was a peace agreement between Israel and Egypt.

★ *Air Force One*: The president flies on a jet called *Air Force One*. It is a Boeing 747-200B that has been modified to meet the president's needs.

Air Force One is the size of a large home. It is equipped with a dining room, sleeping quarters, a conference room, and office space. It also has two kitchens that can provide food for up to 50 people.

★ **The Secret Service:** While not the most glamorous of the president's perks, the Secret Service is one of the most important. The Secret Service is a group of highly trained agents who protect the president and the president's family.

★ **The Presidential State Car:** The presidential limousine is a stretch Cadillac DTS.

It has been armored to protect the president in case of attack. Inside the plush car are a foldaway desk, an entertainment center, and a communications console.

★ **The Food:** The White House has five chefs who will make any food the president wants. The White House also has an extensive wine collection.

★ **Retirement:** A former president receives a pension, or retirement pay, of just under $180,000 a year. Former presidents also receive Secret Service protection for the rest of their lives.

F A C T S

QUALIFICATIONS

To run for president, a candidate must

* ★ be at least 35 years old
* ★ be a citizen who was born in the United States
* ★ have lived in the United States for 14 years

TERM OF OFFICE

A president's term of office is four years.
No president can stay in office for more than two terms.

ELECTION DATE

The presidential election takes place every four years on the first Tuesday of November.

INAUGURATION DATE

Presidents are inaugurated on January 20.

OATH OF OFFICE

I do solemnly swear I will faithfully execute the office of the President of the United States and will to the best of my ability preserve, protect, and defend the Constitution of the United States.

WRITE A LETTER TO THE PRESIDENT

One of the best things about being a U.S. citizen is that Americans get to participate in their government. They can speak out if they feel government leaders aren't doing their jobs. They can also praise leaders who are going the extra mile. Do you have something you'd like the president to do? Should the president worry more about the environment and encourage people to recycle? Should the government spend more money on our schools? You can write a letter to the president to say how you feel!

1600 Pennsylvania Avenue
Washington, D.C. 20500
You can even send an e-mail to: president@whitehouse.gov

BOOKS

Collier, James Lincoln. *The Tecumseh You Never Knew.* New York: Children's Press, 2004.

Doak, Robin S. *William Henry Harrison.* Compass Point Books, 2003.

Feinberg, Barbara Silberdick. *America's First Ladies.* New York: Franklin Watts, 1998.

Hakim, Joy. *From Colonies to Country.* New York: Oxford University Press, 1993.

Schlesinger, Arthur (editor). *The Election of 1840 and the Harrison/Tyler Administrations.* Philadelphia: Mason Crest Publishers, 2003.

VIDEOS

The American President. DVD, VHS (Alexandria, VA: PBS Home Video, 2000).

The History Channel Presents The Presidents. DVD (New York: A & E Home Video, 2005).

The History Channel Presents The War of 1812. DVD (New York: A & E Home Video, 2004).

National Geographic's Inside the White House. DVD (Washington, D.C.: National Geographic Video, 2003).

INTERNET SITES

Visit our Web page for lots of links about William Henry Harrison and other U.S. presidents:

http://www.childsworld.com/links

Note to Parents, Teachers, and Librarians: We routinely verify our Web links to make sure they are safe, active sites—so encourage your readers to check them out!

INDEX